SPELT

A COGNITIVE AND METACOGNITIVE APPROACH TO INSTRUCTION

Strategies
Program
for **E**ffective
Learning
and **T**hinking

Bruce Allen Knight
David Paterson
Robert F. Mulcahy

Acknowledgements

We wish acknowledge the contribution of Dr Bob Mulcahy, Professor of Educational Psychology, University of Alberta, for his key role in the development and ongoing committment to the approach to cognitive and metacognitive instruction described in this book. The SPELT approach is now being effectively implemented in a broad range of learning contexts around the world.

We also wish to acknowledge the artistic skills of Kris Sanotti, Catholic Schools Office, Armidale, for her work in the illustration of this book.

Dedication

We dedicate this book to our wives, Cecily, Janet and Sylvia and to our children for their love and support.

National Library of Australia Cataloguing-in-Publication

Knight, Bruce Allen.
SPELT: a cognitive and metacognitive approach to instruction.

Bibliography.
ISBN 1 86401 722 8.

1. Cognitive learning. 2. Metacognition. 3. Metacognition in children. I. Paterson, David, 1956- II. Mulcahy, R. F.(Robert Frances), 1941-. III. Title. IV. Title: Strategies Program for Effective Learning and Thinking.

370.152

Contents

Introduction

No matter where you reside in Australia, each state and territory's Department of Education has similar aims for its students, i.e. to reach understandings of themselves, to achieve academically, to be a contributing member of society, be independent and be responsible for their own behaviour. These statements reflect, to a greater or lesser extent, the current expectations of the broader community. However, because we live in an age where we are uncertain of what the future holds, there will always be debate about the best type of preparation for individuals to become productive members of society.

The economic and political face of the world continues to change rapidly. The implications of this for employment and leisure are difficult to predict. However, knowledge is expanding at a phenomenal rate and it appears likely that students now in infants schools will undertake two or three major changes in career direction during their working lifetime. This means we need to be looking beyond the development of specific content area knowledge with schools looking to the processes of learning as well as the content.

It is apparent then that autonomous learners will be better prepared for life in a society that is relatively unknown at this stage. Autonomous learning depends on the development of cognitive processes or thinking skills. There has been a considerable amount of research examining those processes (e.g. Sternberg, 1986; Biggs and Telfer, 1987; Borkowski, Carr, Rellinger & Pressley, 1990, Knight and Paterson, 1994) with many programs developed to enhance students' thinking skills (e.g. Marzano and Arredondo (*Tactics for Thinking*), Feurerstein (*Instrumental Enrichment*), Heiman (*Learning to Think*), The Odyssey Project, Mulcahy, Marfo, Peat and Andrews (*SPELT*) and Ashman and Conway (*Process Based Instruction*).

The application of this research on thinking skills to classrooms in Australia, however, is still at an early stage (Ashman and Conway, 1989; Knight and Paterson, 1996; Knight, 1997). Programs and approaches need to be identified which are not only effective but also able to be integrated easily into the activities of the regular classroom.

Section One

INTRODUCTION TO COGNITIVE EDUCATION

The view of learning as a process is based on a constructivist view that learning is an active, constructive process which involves the learners in using and managing their own cognitive processes (Vygotsky, 1978; Harris & Pressley, 1991). Central to this view is the notion that rather than a teacher imparting knowledge, the student constructs it (Biggs and Telfer, 1987). Students are thus actively involved in attending to instruction and their own personal learning in a meaningful way.

A feature of the constructivist view of learning is the notion that cognitive functioning can be modified and enhanced by instruction. Cognitive approaches to education provide a framework to connect three main components of learning: a cognitive component- thinking; a metacognitive component- thinking about thinking; and an affective component- motivation.

It has always been a challenge for a classroom teacher to meet the needs of all students in the one class while teaching within the framework of a curriculum which appears to suggest that certain content has to be mastered at specified times in a student's life. How to develop mastery of content in classes while acknowledging the diversity within those classes is a primary dilemma for teachers. They are faced with the problem of attending to the process of learning within each individual in a way that does not sacrifice mastery of content.

Rather than focusing exclusively on content, the SPELT approach attempts to balance content with process and represents, therefore, an opportunity to develop self-directed learners in the context of regular classroom instruction. As this approach incorporates strategic and affective domains in the development of students as independent learners, the instructional process utilised is of major importance.

The dominant model of cognitive and metacognitive instruction approaches has been teacher imposed where the strategies have been designed by others and taught to students as recipes for dealing with a variety of problems (Mulcahy & Wiles, 1996). In contrast to this, the SPELT approach utilises a model of instruction that actively involves students in generalising strategy use for other situations and in generating, monitoring and evaluating their use of strategies in seeking solutions.

Principal Hallmarks of the SPELT Approach

- Raising students' awareness of their own cognitive processes.
- Guiding students towards control of their own cognitive activities.
- Leading of students towards discovery and deduction.
- Constantly challenging students to be critical, systematic, evaluative and strategic in their behaviour and attitude to learning, thinking and problem solving.

Major Goals of SPELT

For students:

- To become active learners, thinkers and problem solvers.
- To become more planful and strategically efficient in their approach to learning.
- To become independent learners.
- To be aware of, and to control, their own thinking processes (metacognition).

For teachers:

- To develop a working knowledge of the theoretical and applied underpinnings of a learning and thinking strategy program.
- To select and implement strategies that are appropriate for your particular class, and/or school.

COGNITION AND METACOGNITION

Metacognition is considered to have two critical aspects—knowledge and control of cognition. The SPELT approach is concerned with both knowledge and control of cognitive strategies.

Knowledge of Cognitive Strategies

Mulcahy *et al.* (1984:22) define an effective learning strategy as a 'set of processes or steps which facilitate the acquisition, storage and/or utilisation of information'. An individual needs to build a knowledge base of cognitive and metacognitive strategies in order to become a self directed learner. It is essential that students are taught the following types of information:

1. *Declarative knowledge of the strategy.* This includes the factual information about the strategy and its characteristics. For example, students must know that the strategy LEEP has four parts and know what each part of the strategy means.

2. *Procedural knowledge of the strategy.* It is important that learners know the steps involved in applying the strategy. For example, if using the RAP strategy (discussed later in phase one strategies) to improve comprehension, learners need to be aware that firstly they read, then ask a question and finally put it into their own words

3. *Conditional knowledge of when, where and why to apply a strategy.* This knowledge is most important but often neglected. This knowledge is important for generalising strategies to new situations.

Major Components of Control

Control of cognition involves three major components—planning, monitoring and evaluation. To describe the major elements of each, we will use the example of wanting to achieve a high score on a social studies project

1. Planning

Goals   A student's goal for the social studies project is to get an 'A' (90%+) for the project.

Operations   To achieve this result, the student will complete the operations of going to the library early, getting other materials from merchants in the city, writing to companies to get additional information and searching the internet for additional information.

Sequencing   The student will need to set out a timeline which indicates when he will do each of the above operations. For example, go to the library next Tuesday, write letters next weekend, etc.

Obstacles   Potential obstacles that could prevent the student from carrying out his plans include things like football practice, other homework commitments, going away this weekend, no way of getting to the library etc.

Predictions   Involves the student in visualising the situation when he achieves his desired result on the project.

2. Monitoring

Focus   During the monitoring phase, especially when things may not be going to plan, it is important that the student keep the vision and goal in mind.

Sequence   Is the sequence of operations detailed at the planning stage working according to plan?

Subgoals   Keep track of the operations by setting sub-goals such as the collection of information, a time to put all the work together, presentation of information etc.

Selection   Which operations have been successful and which have not.

Obstacles   How will the student overcome obstacles. What if, for example, there are no books left in the library. It is important that the student know how to recover from this and not throw the whole plan away—what alternative sources might provide the information.

3. Evaluation

After the project is completed, it is very important that students evaluate not only the product but also the process that they went through.

Goals   Was the goal or part of the goal achieved?

Results   The student needs to examine the accuracy and adequacy of the result.

Procedures   Which procedures were most effective/least effective. Did the student allow enough time to complete the project? What were the negatives and positives about collecting information and completing the project.

Obstacles   How well and in what manner did the student handle the obstacles?

Plan   Finally the student needs to evaluate the overall plan. Such questions as: were all the steps needed; could he have used different strategies and achieved the same result; what other changes could have been made; may need to be addressed.

CONTROL AND COGNITIVE STRATEGIES

Students' belief systems have also been reported to relate to their metacognitive knowledge and use of strategies (Halmhuber and Paris, 1993; Knight, 1991; 1994; 1995; 1997). It is not only important that students have knowledge of strategies but they also need the motivation to effectively implement them. Alternatively, it is of little use to be motivated to learn but lack any knowledge of strategies . Students' beliefs, expectations and attributions with respect to academic tasks have a major impact on their learning and whether they do become active self-directed learners. This aspect emphasises the bi-directional relationship between metacognitive knowledge and motivational-attitudinal factors.

Locus of Control (LOC)

Students fail their English assignment and offer the following explanations for failure.

> 'I can't do anything right'
> 'School sux'
> 'I spent all of my time doing mathematics'
> 'Mrs P. hates my guts'

These are all examples of either attributing failure to an internal or external LOC. LOC refers to individuals' beliefs about the source of their reinforcements. Reinforcements are viewed as being a consequence of one's own actions and thus under personal internal control or as being unrelated to personal control and due to outside forces such as teachers or peers (external control). Students' behaviours will vary depending upon their expectancies regarding reinforcements received, but it would appear that those with an external LOC have little incentive to invest effort and strive for success. These students will have a generalised expectancy of failure and a concern for avoiding failure rather than striving for success and so there is a need for teachers to be aware of individual students' interpretations of success and failure outcomes and the effects that these can have on the learning process.

For example, if a nine year old girl believes that she will probably get two maths problems out of ten correct, she more than likely won't put in a concerted effort to do her best and in fact might put more effort into thinking of defence mechanism to explain failure rather than using and developing strategies to do the maths work. This situation may occur because the student believes that the teacher sets her hard work rather than that she is not trying or is using inappropriate strategies. If the student does get all the problems correct, then she may believe she got lucky or that the teacher gave her easy work this time. Alternatively, students who believe that success and failure are a consequence of their own behaviour (internal locus of control—active learners) might be expected to show more impetus in intellectual endeavours and general task situations.

Formulation of Specific and Generalised Expectancies

Individual differences in interpretation of reinforcement are highly important contributors to variation in behaviour. As stated, some individuals perceive causal relationships between their own behaviour and its consequences and some do not. As individuals mature, they form beliefs that strengthen expectancies between behaviour and outcomes, and perceptions of the causality of reinforcement form a generalised expectancy (Rotter, 1990).

A generalised expectancy increases in novel situations and decreases as an individual gains more experience in that situation. The development of expectancies (See Figure 1) proceeds through a three stage process:

1. From each of the domains of personal, academic, sports and adaptive behaviour, an individual has a number of experiences in each. Depending upon the outcomes of those experiences, individuals generate an expectancy of receiving reinforcements based on the collective experiences that is domain specific. For example, if a student has a number of humiliating attempts at playing different sports, then the person will probably generate an externalised expectancy regarding a new sporting situation.

2. Each of the expectancies for the different domains formulate into an individual's generalised expectancy. Therefore when faced with a new novel situation, the individual will:

    (a) determine his/her needs and goals; and

    (b) assess the value of receiving reinforcements.

    If the situation is one which has no reinforcement value for the student (e.g. getting a good result for a music project) then the students' LOC orientation is not influential in generating an expectancy of success or failure. If, however, there is high reinforcement value in completing a task (e.g. to be selected on the school's athletic team even if the student believes he is not good at sports), then the student's generalised expectancy of success will be a predictor of success in making the team.

3. These aspects determine the behaviour undertaken, with the strengthening of a generalised expectancy of LOC for future situations in different domains.

Figure 1:   Formulation of Specific and Generalised Expectancies.

(Knight, 1994, after Connolly)

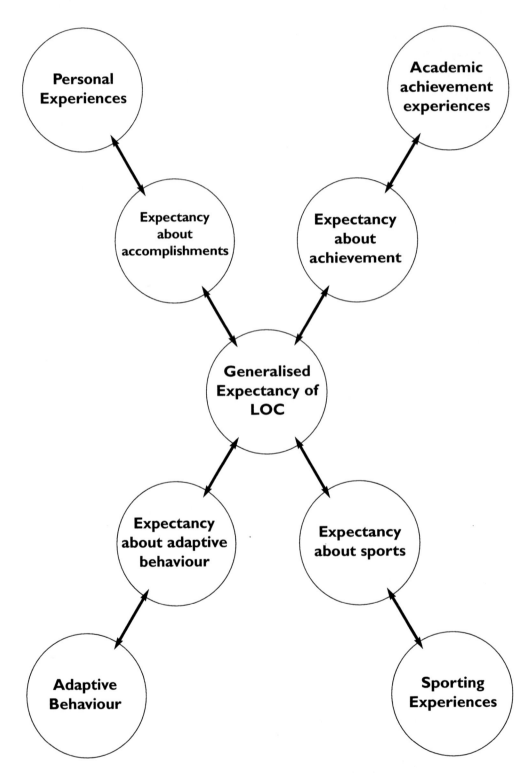

The Failure Cycle

The development of an external LOC expectancy can lead to learned helplessness and a failure cycle (See Figure 2). When students do not perceive events as contingent upon their own behaviour (external LOC), a psychological handicap is generated that thwarts any successful actions from the students themselves and others such as parents and teachers.

Figure 2: Development of an External Locus of Control Expectancy

(Knight, 1994)

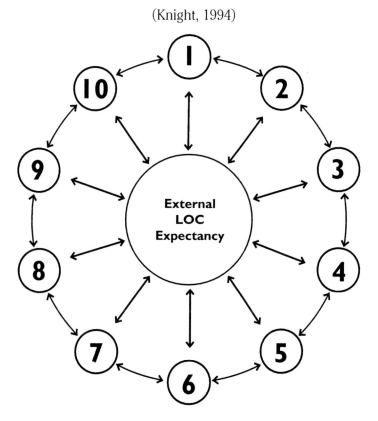

The above diagram will be used to represent how external expectancies develop for Mathematics, which in turn lead to a failure cycle.

1. A student believes that she is not very good at mathematics and therefore does not like the subject.

2. This situation may lead to repeated failure and the student having a lowered estimation of her mathematics and/or general abilities.

3. The student will now have a lowered expectation of success in mathematics.

4. Such a situation leads to underachievement.

5. The student now believes that external factors (e.g. teacher setting hard work, not liking me etc.) control reinforcements and the student avoids doing

mathematics (and thus missing out on valuable practice). Alternatively, any successes will be attributed to luck or the teacher giving easy work, or a peer's help in completing the work.

6. An expectancy of failure is generated as the student becomes more confused leading to a feeling of powerlessness.

7. There is now increased failure as all mathematics may become too difficult and the student hates the subject.

8. Continued failure reinforces to the student a belief in lack of general ability.

9. There is generalised an expectancy to fail to achieve and cope and the student starts to feel bad about herself. A generalised expectancy is generated where she views her reinforcements as being externally controlled and unrelated to her personal behaviour.

10. In the worst case scenario, this can all lead to generalised failure and a failure to cope.

When such a stage of learned helplessness is reached the student believes that outcome is independent of effort. It is important then that teachers become involved in attributional retraining (making students aware of their own effort in the learning process) which involves students in making more 'favourable' causal attributions rather than saying 'I'm just dumb' or 'its too hard' etc. This is best achieved by firstly teaching students strategies and then by having them attribute failure to insufficient effort by not using a strategy (something they can control) or inefficient use of a strategy. Each occasion for strategy instruction is also an opportunity for retraining students' negative attributions.

Dual-Dimensional View of Locus of Control

Wong and Sproule (1984) have proposed a dual-dimensional view of LOC (where internal and external control are two separate dimensions) as opposed to Rotter's unidimensional view where internal and external control are opposing tendencies on a single dimension. Rather than a model of internal versus external LOC, Wong and Sproule propose internal *and* external LOC or dual control. Hence dual control does not absolve an individual of personal responsibility, but rather the advantages of dual control are recognised. External control can be positive wherein teachers work with students in their 'zone of proximal development' (Vygotsky, 1978). An example of this in action is the work of reading recovery teachers when they work with a student at his/her instructional level.

The established findings that students with an internal LOC are superior to students with an external LOC in a variety of tasks are not questioned, nor is the importance of personal control. What is suggested is that by positively assisting failing students through dual control they will become more active, independent learners.

METACOGNITIVE LEARNERS

Students with well developed metacognitive skills tend to be more effective learners and display certain characteristics when compared with students who are 'non-metacognitive'.

- Active Learning

    Effective learners are self-questioning and summarise their knowledge and understanding of a topic. Less effective learners adopt a more passive learning approach and tend not to interact with the material. Teacher dominated approaches are likely to reinforce passive learning.

- Internal Locus of Control

    Effective learners tend to have a more internal locus of control and be more self-directed learners (see section of locus of control for further discussion of this construct). Ineffective learners, because of their passive approach to learning, believe that they are not responsible for the outcomes of their behaviour and that their learning is controlled by the teacher.

- Strategy Efficient

    Effective learners know and use a range of efficient strategies. They know when, where and why these strategies should be used. Less effective learners are either strategy deficient or strategy inefficient (e.g. tend to use one strategy for many tasks regardless of its effectiveness).

- Reflective

    Effective learners are those who are reflective in their approach to solving problems, rather than impulsive. Impulsivity is usually encouraged by teachers when they ask closed questions that require an immediate answer. We need also to encourage students to relect on tasks and be aware of choices by perhaps asking more open-ended questions.

Development of SPELT: Some Theoretical Influences

Development of the SPELT approach has been influenced by research in the area of intelligence and intelligent behaviour. Theoretical models and concepts developed by Robert Sternberg, Art Costa, Donald Dansereau, and Joseph Rigney have been particularly influential in this regard. In the following pages, we consider some key features of these models.

Sets of Learning and Thinking Skills: Sternberg

The work of Sternberg is significant because of his conceptualisation of intelligence as a set of teachable learning and thinking skills.

- Problem identification

    This is the most important prerequisite to successful problem solving. It is essential that students define the problem accurately and not set up barriers that they believe are inherent to the problem and its solution.

- Process selection

  Students select processes that are appropriate to the problem or task at hand.

- Representation selection

  This involves the student in selecting useful ways of representing information pertaining to the task both internally (in one's head) and externally (for example, on paper).

- Strategy selection

  Involves the selection of sequences in which to apply processes to representation.

- Processing allocation

  Efficient allocation of time to various aspects or components of a task. If students are required to do a project, for example, they would be encouraged to allocate time and resources in such a manner that the project can be completed in the most efficient and effective manner.

- Solution monitoring

  Involves students in keeping track of what has been done, what remains to be done, and whether satisfactory progress is being made

- Sensitivity to feedback

  Students must use feedback to improve their performance on a task.

- Translation of feedback into action plan

  This is necessary so that students not only to know what they are doing incorrectly, but most importantly to use the knowledge gained in a plan of corrective action.

- Implementation of the action plan

  Quite often learners may know what has to be done but they fail to carry through the plan. It is critical that students be motivated to implement their plans.

Intelligent Behaviours: Costa

Feurerstein (1980) has suggested that evidence of the following behaviours outlined by Costa can be used as data to indicate that students are behaving intelligently. These attributes are encouraged in the SPELT teaching methodology.

- Persevering when a solution to a problem is not immediately apparent. Rather than giving in to a task, students are encouraged to analyse and use strategies to solve problems.

- Decreasing impulsivity. Students are encouraged to reflect on gathered information and plan strategies for solving problems.

- Developing flexibility in thinking. This encourages students to consider alternative viewpoints and be concerned with the process of problem-solving.

Rather than presenting problems requiring right/wrong answers, teachers are encouraged to set open-ended problems that allow students to listen to others' viewpoints and evaluate different methods of achieving the same result.

- Metacognition involves students in becoming aware of their own thinking and control over their learning processes. When metacognitive, students can clarify and evaluate the steps involved in their approaches to solving a problem.

- Checking for accuracy and precision is a skill which encourages students to reflect upon their work. Too often students use the quickest method to finish a task and promptly exclaim finished when they find an answer. Students need to be encouraged to check their work for its accuracy and clarity by using appropriate strategies.

- Questioning and problem posing. It is more difficult to formulate the questions rather than write the answers.

- Drawing on past knowledge and applying it to new situations. Students need to relate previous experiences to the next experience.

- Inquisitiveness, curiosity, and the enjoyment of problem solving . We need students to have not only the 'I can do this attitude', but also to enjoy the challenge.

Classes of Strategies : Dansereau

Donald Dansereau (1985) developed a framwork for describing cognitive and metacognitive strategies which is used in the SPELT instructional approach. Dansereau identified two broad classes of strategies—primary and support. This book contains examples of both kinds of strategies.

- Primary:

  Primary strategies are used by students to work directly with the material. Examples of primary strategies include phase I strategies such as RAP and COPS (discussed later) which relate directly to reading comprehension and the editing of writing.

- Support:

  Support strategies are concerned with the affective component of instruction, an often neglected but vital area. These strategies ensure that the primary strategies flow efficiently and effectively by ensuring the learner and his/her environment get maximum value for learning. An example of a support strategy which is discussed later in the book is the BRAG strategy.

Approaches to Teaching: Rigney

The framework for the SPELT instructional model was strongly influenced by a theoretical model developed by Joseph W. Rigney (1978). This model, discussed below, relates to students' use of cognitive strategies or ways of performing learning tasks in instructional situations. The model (Figure 3) represents instruction in terms of two dimensions—control of strategy initiation and explicitness of strategy. The four quadrants represent four different instructional situations.

Figure 3: Approaches to Teaching and Using Cognitive Strategies
(Rigney, 1978)

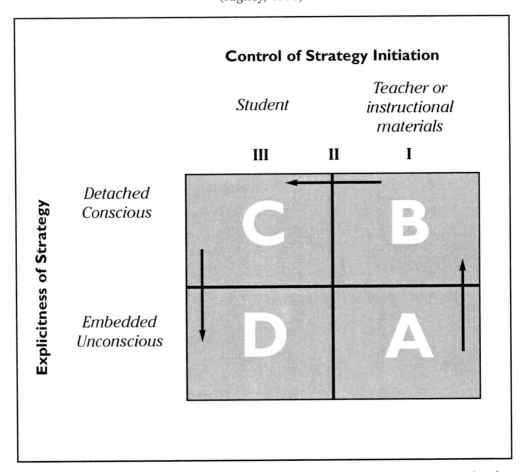

Control of strategy initiation refers to the source or cue for strategy use; who (or what) decides under which circumstances a strategy is to be used? This may be either the student or the teacher/instructional material. Explicitness of strategy concerns the degree to which a cognitive strategy may be described independently of the subject material.

Quadrant A represents the most common situation in classrooms. Here the initiation of cognitive strategies is controlled either by the teacher or by the instructional material. Those cognitive strategies are embedded in the learning task and the learner is usually not conscious of their presence. One example of this would be a school textbook. A strategy for finding information in such a textbook is actually embedded in the material itself; there exists a system of headings and subheadings, contents and indices, boxes and shading, which are designed for the specific purpose of assisting the learner to find information. Unfortunately for some learners, however, this system or strategy for finding information has never been drawn to their attention and they may be simply unaware of it. For them, the textbook may consist of many pages covered with text. In another example, a teacher may impose a cognitive strategy of self-monitoring on learners by asking them to put up their hand when they have finished a worksheet. The task has been constructed by the teacher in such a way as to require learners to use the strategy if they are to succeed. Unfortunately, however, some learners may be unaware of the strategy and be using the self-monitoring strategy (efficiently or not) in an unconscious manner. If the teacher then asked a learner to describe how they knew when to put their hand up, some may be unable to do so.

In **Quadrant B** initiation of cognitive strategies is still controlled by either the teacher or the instructional material. The significant change from the situation in Quadrant A, however, is that the learner is now conscious of those cognitive strategies. They are now detached from the task and able to be described independently of the task. In this situation the student is now able to see and talk about the information-finding strategy built into the design of the textbook. Initiation of the strategy, however, is still controlled by the design of the material; it would be unlikely that the student would use a different strategy to find information in that textbook. Similarly the student asked to raise their hand when finished is, in the Quadrant B situation, now aware of the mental operations they are performing and would be able to describe them independently of the task. The nature of the teacher's request, however, means that control for initiation of the strategy still remains with the teacher.

Quadrant C represents a major shift. Here the student consciously assumes control of strategy initiation. The strategy is still considered in an explicit manner detached from the task or subject material but this time the student chooses to either initiate the strategy or not. An example of this might be a situation in which a student is required to memorise some information. The student may be able to describe and use a variety of different strategies to perform this task but chooses to use a strategy in which they visualise the information. This choice will depend on a range of factors relating to themselves (how they feel at the time, their beliefs about learning etc), the task (is it hard? easy? meaningful?), or to the strategy (whether it usually works, requires effort to implement etc).

Quadrant D, finally, is a situation which is believed to be a goal for the development of self-directed learners. Here the control for initiation of cognitive strategies is with the student but the choices being made to engage particular strategies under different circumstances are made 'subconsciously'. The strategy being used is now embedded in the task or subject material and cannot be readily described independently of that task. A good example of this situation can be seen if you ask a friend to describe how they remember a telephone number. While the choice to perform this strategy is clearly made by the learner, it has become so automatic that it is difficult to bring to conscious attention and describe independently of the task.

Rigney (1978) noted that from a learning perspective Quadrant A represented the current situation for many students and that while Quadrant C was a desirable situation, it could only be realised by first implementing the situation represented in Quadrant B.

THE SPELT INSTRUCTIONAL MODEL

The SPELT Instructional Model is based on the conceptual framework presented by Rigney in the model described above. Major goals for SPELT instruction outlined earlier include the development of learners who are planful, strategic, independent and interdependent; the situation described in Quadrants C and D of Rigney's model. To achieve this in the classroom, however, it is necessary to facilitate the progression of student learning from the Quadrant A situation through Quadrant B to the situation represented by Quadrant C. Progression to Quadrant D is then believed to be dependent on the student and contextual variables such as amount of practice.

Figure 4: The SPELT Instructional Model

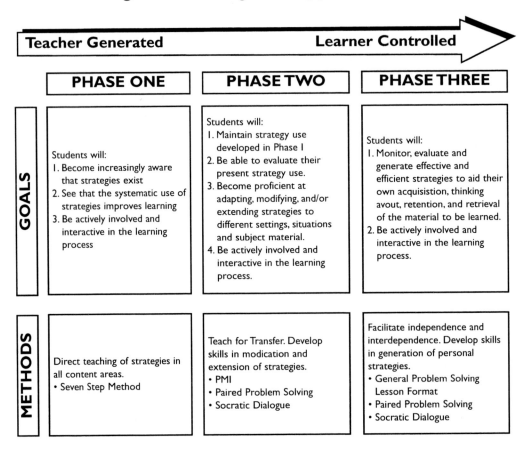

SPELT: A Cognitive/Metacognitive Approach to Instruction

	PHASE ONE	**PHASE TWO**	**PHASE THREE**
GOALS	Students will: 1. Become increasingly aware that strategies exist 2. See that the systematic use of strategies improves learning 3. Be actively involved and interactive in the learning process	Students will: 1. Maintain strategy use developed in Phase I 2. Be able to evaluate their present strategy use. 3. Become proficient at adapting, modifying, and/or extending strategies to different settings, situations and subject material. 4. Be actively involved and interactive in the learning process.	Students will: 1. Monitor, evaluate and generate effective and efficient strategies to aid their own acquisition, thinking avout, retention, and retrieval of the material to be learned. 2. Be actively involved and interactive in the learning process.
METHODS	Direct teaching of strategies in all content areas. • Seven Step Method	Teach for Transfer. Develop skills in modication and extension of strategies. • PMI • Paired Problem Solving • Socratic Dialogue	Facilitate independence and interdependence. Develop skills in generation of personal strategies. • General Problem Solving Lesson Format • Paired Problem Solving • Socratic Dialogue

The SPELT Model can be described as an instructional continuum from teacher generated to student controlled learning. Instruction in this Model begins at Phase One and progresses to Phase Three.

A general teaching orientation embedded in SPELT actively involves students in their own learning. The teacher acts as a facilitator in enhancing students' awareness of their own cognitive and metacognitive processes and of their motives in learning. Within this orientation, students are challenged to be critical, evaluative and strategic in their behaviour and attitude towards learning.

There are two types of instructional methodologies used in the SPELT approach to promote independent learning. Firstly, in phase one, direct instruction is used to teach learning strategies. During this teacher-dominated phase, the teacher identifies strategies (or generates them in consultation with students) to use in solving problems directly related to the classroom such content or student behaviour.

A second methodology, predominantly used in phases two and three, emphasises the use of dialogue and individual/group instruction (cooperative learning and co-construction of appropriate strategies) to enhance students' transfer and generalisation of strategies to other situations. The use of socratic dialogue in working with students in their 'zone of proximal development' (Vygotsky, 1978) is used to facilitate students' learning. This practice is similar to an apprenticeship type model where both teacher and student work together to achieve results. Students are encouraged to 'think aloud' so that teachers can reinforce an awareness of strategies to be used and also guide students thinking toward the use of strategies to solve different problems. These practices lead ultimately to the student generating their own strategies and independence in their learning.

Phase One

Phase One corresponds with the situation described by Quadrant B of Rigney's model in which initiation of cognitive strategies is controlled by either the teacher or the instructional material. The student, however, is conscious of those cognitive strategies. This phase involves the direct teaching of strategies relevant to the teachers' program and is thus teacher dominated. The strategies are identified or generated by the teacher.

Goals of this phase include making students aware of and the benefits of strategic behaviour and the development of a bank of strategies. This phase is also an opportunity to develop self-confidence and positive attributional beliefs leading to the development of an internal LOC.

If is important however that instruction not stop in this teacher dominated phase, as students will remain passive and perceive an external LOC orientation. If the teacher is always providing strategies and students are not evaluating their use nor generating their own, they are still reliant on the teacher for support.

Phase Two

Phase Two, corresponds with the critical transition between Quadrants B and C. A range of instructional methods are used to facilitate a shift in control for initiation of strategies from the teacher to the student while those strategies are still being described in a conscious and explicit manner. Thus this phase is concerned with transfer and generalisation. The instruction focus moves away from the teacher to be one of more interaction with students. Students, using dialogue in cooperative learning situations with their peers and teachers, are encouraged to analyse and evaluate their use of strategies. Students are made aware that strategies that are presented to them by the teacher are not the be all and end all of their learning with students encouraged to modify strategies to suit their own purposes. This personalisation of strategies allows students to develop deeper understanding of tasks, strategies and thus influences their beliefs regarding control and their own learning.

Phase Three

Phase Three corresponds with the situation described by Quadrant C of Rigney's model. The student consciously assumes control of strategy initiation while those cognitive strategies can still be considered in a conscious and explicit manner. This phase of instruction, involving minimal teacher guidance, enables students to draw upon the strategic and conditional knowledges developed in earlier phases. Students use this knowledge to generate their own strategies to solve problems and complete tasks. Paired and group problem solving, where students are encouraged to 'think aloud', is utilised to enable students to describe how a task is approached and to monitor and evaluate the use of strategies to complete the task. We believe this represents a situation in which the student can be described as a self-directed learner, a goal of schools and educational systems.

Section Two

In this section we shall present in some detail ways in which the SPELT instructional approach should be implemented.

PHASE ONE INSTRUCTION

It is in the first phase of instruction in the SPELT model that the teacher assumes the greatest greatest control of instruction and teaches in a direct and explicit manner. While this usually results in significant short-term improvement for students, teachers must be conscious of the real risks involved in instruction which is controlled and directed only by the teacher. Unless the teacher moves rapidly to Phase Two instruction, students may become increasingly dependent on the teacher, a situation which is clearly contrary to the aims of the SPELT approach.

The Goals of Phase One

Students will:

- Become increasingly aware that strategies exist.
- See that systematic use of strategies improves learning.
- Be actively involved and interactive in the learning process

What this means for student and teacher

- Become increasingly aware that strategies exist.

  Students in this Phase of instruction need to become more metacognitively aware. Awareness that such things as learning strategies actually exist at all and can be described is a critical first step if a student is to become a more strategic learner.

- See that systematic use of strategies improves learning.

  Knowing that strategies exist is necessary but not sufficient. Students need to understand that learning in a more systematic and strategic way will have some immediate personal benefit—there must be a reason for a student to change the way they learn. The teacher's role is to clearly illustrate that this will be the case.

- Be actively involved and interactive in the learning process

   This is a common goal across the three Phases of instruction. At all times students must be cognitively active participants in their own learning; comparing new and existing knowledge, practicing new strategies, constructing new understandings.

Phase One Instructional Methods

Seven Step Method

Step One: Motivation and measurement base

The students engage in a moderately difficult task which requires the use of the target strategy. Performance is measured and recorded. The teacher presents the results of this measurement to illustrate need for improvement.

Step Two: Sell-job

Based on the results of measurement conducted in Step One, the teacher 'sells' the notion of learning a strategy which will improve performance.

The target strategy is then described in detail and explained.

Step Three: Modelling

The teacher models use of the target strategy with an appropriate task.

Step Four: Drill for memorisation

Students systematically memorise the steps involved in the target strategy using rapidly paced verbal rehearsal drills. Visual cues may be used but should be withdrawn as quickly as possible.

Step Five: Practice

Students practice using the target strategy with instructional material selected by the teacher. Material must be easy and be an appropriate task in which the target strategy can be used.

Step Six: Feedback

While the students are practicing use of the target strategy the teacher gives appropriate feedback; positive or corrective. Feedback relates to the students' use of the strategy, not performance on the selected task.

Step Seven: Post-test

In a similar manner to Step One, students engage in a moderately difficult task which requires the use of the target strategy. Performance is again measured and recorded. In presenting the results of this measurement to students the teacher compares current performance with performance prior to learning the target strategy. Improvement in task performance is used as an illustration of the value of systematic use of a strategy.

What this Means for Student and Teacher

The seven-step method described above will be recognised by teachers as a synthesis of a considerable body of knowledge about effective teaching. It is not a 'new' instructional method but a sequence which has been shown to be effective for the rapid acquisition of new skills.

Step One is designed to obtain some baseline measurement of performance against which change can be measured. While recording should be done in a way that can be readily understood by the students, the method chosen will depend on the task. A second purpose for Step One is to illustrate to students that there is room for improvement in their performance of a specified task. The teacher must be careful in subsequent discussion to maintain a focus on that particular task and on the strategies for completing that task. At this stage of instruction teachers should be aware of the risk of some students becoming discouraged about their performance and challenge this by moving briskly to the next step.

Step Two is the time for the teacher to enthusiastically present a way to improve individual performance which is both novel and likely to be effective. Prior to explanation of the strategy the teacher should emphasise that use of the strategy is a 'better way' and 'more efficient'. The notion of more efficient use of time and effort should be stressed to avoid the possibility that students may see strategy use as simply a more complicated and effortful way of failing.

Detailed explanation of the strategy, including reasons for each step, helps the student know that understanding of the strategy, not just rote memorisation, are necessary. In addition, such explanation sends to students a message that the teacher intends to be explicit about instruction and expects active involvement from the student.

Step Three involves the teacher actually modelling use of the strategy with an appropriate task. Thinking aloud is a key feature of this modelling in which the teacher says out load what would be going on in his/her head during application of the strategy. This is necessary to make operation of the strategy clear to the student. In addition, the student sees the teacher as a strategic learner rather than a container of knowledge.

Step Four involves memorisation of steps in the strategy using verbal rehearsal drills. This memory step necessarily follows previous steps in which the reasons for the strategy have been explained. Students need to be able to quickly and easily remember the new strategy so that subsequently, when the strategy needs to be engaged, cognitive effort can be spent using the strategy, not remembering particular steps within it.

Teachers may find that verbal rehearsal drills need to be accompanied by use of a visual aid. If this is necessary, the aid should be withdrawn as soon as strategy steps can be retrieved from memory both quickly and accurately.

Step Five is a crucial step in which students begin to use the strategy. It must be stressed that for this initial application of the strategy, the material selected by the teacher must be easy. Students are practising using a new strategy and their attention should be on this task. The aim here is not to confuse students by requiring them to also understand difficult subject material. If a teacher is in doubt as to the relative difficulty of a task for any student in this instructional step it is far better to provide material which the student believes to be ridiculously simple!

Step Six takes place simultaneously with Step Five as the students are practicing use of the new strategy. Because Step Five involves practice which is guided by the teacher, the feedback provided enables the student to learn how to use the strategy most effectively. Teacher feedback relates not to the mastery of the (simple) task but to use of the new strategy. Positive feedback (e.g. 'You remembered the first step of the strategy and seem to be applying it correctly.') can be given for appropriate strategy use. If aspects of strategy use are inappropriate, corrective feedback (e.g. 'What was the third step?… OK… Try it again.') can be given. If strategy steps are forgotten, the teacher may need to return to verbal rehearsal practiced in Step Four.

Step Seven is the final step in this instructional method. Here the teacher engages the students in a task similar to that presented in Step One. It would be expected that the progression from Step One to Step Seven should be relatively rapid in order that students remember the way in which they performed the task initially. The significant difference in the way students now perform this task should relate to use of the new, target strategy. Improvement in task performance should be made obvious by the teacher and it should be stressed that this improvement can be attributed to strategy use by the students, not to any change in the task or assistance from the teacher.

In the event that performance does not change significantly, teachers may begin the instructional cycle again with a different strategy or choose to examine, with the student, some ways that use of the strategy could be refined.

Examples of Strategies

In the following pages, a few examples are presented of strategies which might be introduced during Phase One instruction and which have been effectively used by students. It must be stressed that these are examples only, the range of strategies can be as varied as the range of learners and learning situations.

1. RAP

PARAPHRASING STRATEGIES

Purpose of Strategy

The purpose of this strategy is to aid in the comprehension of written material. Can be used by students to help remember more of what has been read, particularly for detailed material or that which is abstract. Also useful for note taking and studying.

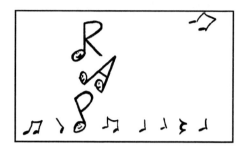

Description of Strategy

This is a • Task specific,
           • Primary strategy

R	Read	Read the paragraph silently yourself.
A	Ask	After reading the paragraph, ask yourself what you have just read. (Does it make sense? How does it relate to what I already know? How does it relate to what I have already read? What is the main idea the author is trying to get across? What are two supporting details?)
P	Put it in your own words	Write notes based on what has been read and asked about putting the main idea and two details in your own words.

Teaching Example

Present to students with a piece of written material, asking them to try to remember what they've read. The next day, ask them to answer comprehension questions based on this piece of written material. Keep scores of their performance. After RAP has been taught, students are given another piece of written material and asked to RAP it. The comprehension questions are asked again the next day. A comparison of scores should illustrate for students the effectiveness of RAP for improving both comprehension and retention.

RAP could be expanded to include the concepts of 'main idea' and 'supporting details'.

(Source: Alley and Deshler, 1979.)

2. RIDER

VISUAL IMAGERY STRATEGY

Purpose of Strategy

Comprehension of written material. Can be used by students to help remember more of what has been read, particularly narrative and descriptive material.

R
I
D
E
R

Description of Strategy

This is a • Task specific,
          • Primary strategy

R	Read	Read a sentence or short section of text.
I	Imagine	Imagine a picture of what you've just read.
D	Describe	Describe this picture to yourself.
E	Elaborate	Elaborate this picture; including details of clothing, colours, movement, setting etc.
R	Repeat	Repeat the previous steps, gradually changing the original picture (e.g. like frames in a movie).

Teaching Example

Before teaching the RIDER strategy, give students a descriptive passage, instructing them to read it silently. As they read, circulate around the classroom, asking individual students 'what do you see?'

Encourage detailed images by asking students to close their eyes and visualise (elaborate on) the colours, type of clothing, movements, setting etc.

(Source: Adapted from Alley and Deshler, 1979.)

3. COPS

SELF CORRECTION STRATEGY

Purpose of Strategy

This strategy helps student to edit or correct their own writing. It can be used for proofreading their own writing after completion of a rough draft or for checking of other students' work prior to handing in. The strategy may also be used for proof reading essay exam questions.

Description of Strategy

This is a • Task specific,
  • Primary strategy

Students read through the piece of writing four times, checking each time for only one aspect as represented by the COPS mnemonic.

A system of editing rules could be used by the class as COPS is being implemented on the piece of writing.

C	Capitals	Do the first words in each sentence and proper nouns begin with capital letters?
O	Overall appearance	How is the overall appearance and readability (i.e. spacing, legibility, neatness, complete sentences etc)
P	Punctuation	Is the punctuation correct?
S	Spelling	Are all the words spelled correctly?

Teaching Example

This strategy could be introduced to a class or individual students who do not effectively edit or conference drafts of written work. 'Before' and 'after' examples of written work corrected before introduction of COPS could be compared with examples of work corrected using the COPS strategy. The teacher should draw students' attention to the degree of improvement in written work following use of the COPS strategy.

(Source: Adapted from Alley and Deshler, 1979.)

4. CARING

LISTENING STRATEGY

Purpose of Strategy

This strategy can be used to help systematically clarify what is meant by listening behaviour during a teacher or student presentation to the class.

Description of Strategy

This is a • Task specific,
  • Support strategy

C	Cares about the message	Tune in to the message and think about the feelings of the speaker.
A	Always looks at the speaker	Keep eyes on the person or people speaking.
R	Remains comfortably seated	Don't fidget or move around.
I	Is quiet	Don't make any noise while someone is speaking to you
N	Notices detail	Pay attention to detail so that questions or replies can be formulated.
G	Greets speaker with an open mind	Try to think only about what is being said.

Teaching Example

This strategy could be introduced if, during an oral presentation, some students are not attending (i.e. not caring about the presentation, chattering to each other, moving about, engaging in other work). Introduction of the strategy would follow a discussion about what it feels like to talk to a group of people who appear uninterested and the possible consequences for both speaker and listener.

5. LEEP

ORAL REPORT PRESENTATION STRATEGY

Purpose of Strategy

This strategy has been developed to help students remember behaviours which will assist in clear and meaningful oral presentations.

Description of Strategy

This is a • Task specific,
           • Primary strategy

L	Loud and clear	Use a sufficiently loud voice and speak clearly to enable the audience to hear and understand what you are saying.
E	Expression	Use interesting expression, pitch and tone, in your voice.
E	Eye contact	Make eye contact with your audience.
P	Posture	Stand or sit in such a way as to show that you're interested in what you're saying; lean forward sometimes, don't slouch.

Teaching Example

Students could be encouraged to be in the audience of an oral presentation by a skilled presenter or to watch a videotape of such a presentation. This could be used as a stimulus after which techniques used by the presenter could be discussed. Presentation of the LEEP strategy could follow as a summary of those techniques.

6. STAR

CREATIVE WRITING STRATEGY

Purpose of Strategy

This strategy can be used as a brainstorming technique for the generation of ideas before beginning to write. It may also be used as a working outline for the writing of a short story.

Description of Strategy

This is a • Task specific,
              • Primary strategy

Using the following format, students generate an outline as the beginning of a writing process.

S	Setting	The setting describes the place or characters.
T	Trouble or problem	What is the trouble or problem which will be described in your story?
A	Action	Describe the actions which will take place.
R	Results	What will be the results at the end of your story?

Teaching Example

Distribute a package of jumbled paper strips to each student or group of students, with a part of a passage of writing on each strop. Ask your students to categorise the strips according to setting, trouble (or problem), action and results. This should illustrate to students that pieces of writing are often generated in this fashion. The STAR mnemonic can then be introduced to summarise this strategy.

7. LOCI

MEMORY STRATEGY

Purpose of Strategy

This strategy assists students to remember apparently disconnected words or ideas. This strategy is particularly useful when order is important in either forward or reverse sequence. It can be used as an aid for remembering key points in an oral presentation, using the visual setting of the presentation as a cue for retrieval.

Loci

Description of Strategy

This is a • Task specific,
          • Primary strategy

In this strategy visual imagery is used to link items to be remembered with items in familiar settings. Location of items in students' homes or different rooms could serve as settings.

Step One	Take a visual walk	Let your eyes move in one direction around a familiar setting. Choose visually distinctive items from that setting.
Step Two	Link the items	Visualise the items to be remembered as either a part of or on the distinctive item.
Step Three	Rehearse and say	Again, let your eyes move in one direction around the familiar setting. As you observe the distinctive item, retrieve from memory and say the item to be remembered.
Step Four	Rehearse	Let your eyes move in one direction around the familiar setting—try reversing direction. This time, as you observe the distinctive item, retrieve the item to be remembered from memory but say it to yourself.

Teaching Example

Number familiar classroom items as you walk around the circumference of the room (e.g. 1–blackboard, 2–door, 3–noticeboard etc). Present students with a list of items to be remembered drawn from the current lesson. Have the students take an imaginary walk around the room visualising the items to be remembered as part of the familiar classroom objects previously numbered. Take the imaginary walk several times until the visual image is very clear. The following day, instruct students to again take the visual walk around the room retrieving the items learned as they do so. This should illustrate to students the effectiveness of this strategy.

This strategy could be used to improve responsible behaviour by having the students:

• visualise a walk from (for example) the classroom, along corridors, to playground.

• speak, as they visualise, the responsibilities connected with each location (e.g. clearing desk, walking quietly, playing by the rules)

8. BRAG

RELAXATION STRATEGY

Purpose of Strategy

This strategy is designed to help students relax and break the book-anxiety-day-dreaming cycle. It can be used during many anxiety-producing situations such as preparation for an examination or prior to a presentation.

Description of Strategy

This is a • Task specific,
          • Support strategy

B	Breathe deeply and slowly	Be aware of your body. Sit comfortably and concentrate on your breathing.
R	Relax all muscles	Be aware of your body. Tense then slowly relax each muscle group for a count of ten.
A	Allow brief visualisation	Visualise a pleasant setting, one which you associate with feelings of pleasure, calmness and relaxation.
G	Go back to task	Visualise yourself moving back to the target activity. Because you are still relaxed, you should feel no anxiety or tension. Now get up and begin to work.

Teaching Example

Relaxation processes can be introduced to a class by leading students through a cycle of body awareness (breathing, tension and relaxation of muscle groups) and visualisation. Once the feeling of 'relaxation' is identified, the BRAG strategy can be introduced for students to use when they feel themselves becoming tense.

9. ODD

EMOTIONAL AWARENESS STRATEGY

OWN DEGREE OF DISCOMFORT

Purpose of Strategy

This strategy is designed to help students develop an awareness of the differing degrees of their own emotional discomfort in a variety of situations. In addition to increasing awareness and discernment of emotions within self and others it can be used to assist students understand that people see situations with differing degrees of emotion. This insight could subsequently be used as a mechanism to develop self-control in a variety of situations.

Description of Strategy

This is a: • Task specific,
                    • Support strategy

A drawing of a thermometer with a scale of 0 to 100 is used by students to concretely represent their own degree of discomfort (ODD) felt in different situations.

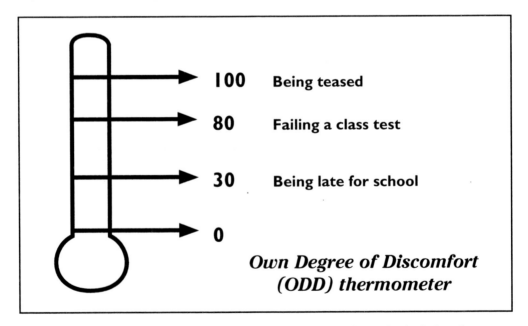

100	**Being teased**
80	**Failing a class test**
30	**Being late for school**
0	

*Own Degree of Discomfort
(ODD) thermometer*

This strategy would normally be used when considering hypothetical situations, not while actually experiencing the emotional discomfort. Students would gradually be taught to internally represent their emotions on a scale and recognise stressful situations.

Teaching Example.

Hypothetical problem situations may be presented to students (i.e. being teased, not being invited to a party) and a response modelled by the teacher ('When I get teased it makes me feel sort of angry but when I'm not invited to a party that all my friends are going to, I feel very sad'). The ODD thermometer would then be presented as a way to represent the ranking of the 'degree of discomfort' discussed above.

Initially, different thermometers could represent various emotions generated by the students. Eventually, one thermometer could be used to represent general emotional level (i.e. anger, happiness, excitement, fear, anxiety, feelings towards school subjects etc).

When students are able to use the ODD thermometer in a group discussion, individual thermometers could be made and compared.

A large poster size thermometer with a sliding scale made for both teacher and student use could facilitate understanding of each others emotions with regard to particular situations. An outcome of discussions and use of the ODD thermometer is to generate (see Phase Three) or identify need for strategies to deal with negative emotions which are identified.

(Source: Adapted from Rotheram, 1978.)

10. IDEA DIAGRAM
WRITING OUTLINE STRATEGY

Purpose of Strategy

The purpose of this strategy is to provide an organising framework which will guide students' observations and assist in the preparation of an outline from which to write. The strategy is particularly suited for use as a brainstorming technique. It can be used for report writing, note-taking, creative writing or for providing a framework for studying.

A similar framework could be provided to organise students' information, thoughts, and actions in social settings as an aid for anticipating different behaviours required in a variety of social contexts.

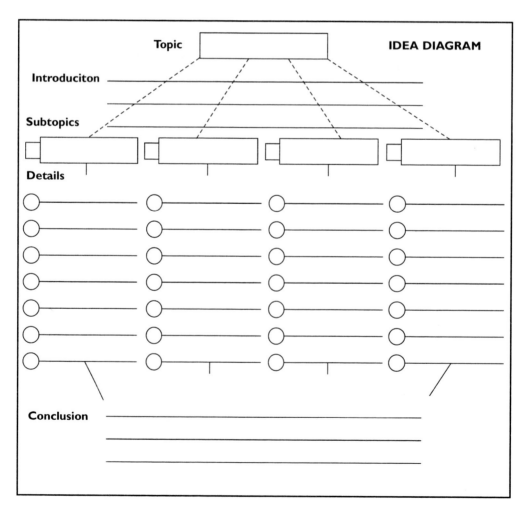

Description of Strategy

This is a • Task specific,
            • Primary strategy

Students use the diagram provided and fill in, using only a few words, the organising sections listed. Students write down ideas in any order within the appropriate sections. Small squares (attached to 'subtopic' rectangles) and circles (attached to 'details' lines) are filled in after brainstorming to establish order.

Teaching Example

Have students fill out an outline of a report on a famous person. Students can then be shown how to write two reports from the same outline; one in chronological order, one in order of 'most important contribution of person' to 'least important contribution of person'.

The Idea Diagram may be used to structure brainstorming of ideas before a new social situation arises or to aid analysis of a social situation after the fact. Before use relates to issues such as thinking about and preparing for new situations, sequencing behaviour, discussion of possible outcomes of behaviour etc. After use aids social analysis in order to formulate future other options/behaviour leading to new and better consequences. The Idea Diagram could also help to sequence the priority order of dealing with identified social problems.

(Source: Alley and Deshler, 1979.)

11.RAT

PARAPHRASING STRATEGY

Purpose of Strategy

The purpose of this strategy is to assist in the comprehension of written material. Can be used by students to help remember more of what has been read, particularly for detailed material or that which is abstract. Also useful for note taking and studying.

Description of Strategy

This is a • Task specific,
            • Primary strategy

RAT is a modification of the RAP paraphrasing strategy, using a more explicit writing step.

R	Read	Read the paragraph silently yourself.
A	Ask	After reading the paragraph, ask yourself what you have just read. (Does it make sense? How does it relate to what I already know? How does it relate to what I have already read? What is the main idea the author is trying to get across? What are two supporting details?)
T	Tell	Tell yourself (or a partner) answers to the questions you have asked.

Teaching Example

Present to students with a piece of written material, asking them to try to remember what they've read. The next day, ask them to answer comprehension questions based on this piece of written material. Keep scores of their performance. The next day, ask them to answer comprehension questions based on this piece of written material. Keep scores of their performance. After RAT has been taught, students are given another piece of written material and asked to RAT it. The comprehension questions are asked again the next day. A comparison of scores should illustrate for students the effectiveness of RAT for improving both comprehension and retention.

(Source: Kris Sanotti, St Edward's School, Tamworth)

12. RAD

PARAPHRASING STRATEGY

Purpose of Strategy

The purpose of this strategy is to assist in the comprehension of written material. Can be used by students to help remember more of what has been read, particularly for detailed material or that which is abstract. This strategy is suitable for younger students or students who do not have well-developed writing skills.

Description of Strategy

This is a • Task specific,
          • Primary strategy

RAD is a modification of the RAP paraphrasing strategy, using a drawing in place of a writing step.

R	Read	Read the paragraph silently yourself.
A	Ask	After reading the paragraph, ask yourself what you have just read. (Does it make sense? How does it relate to what I already know? How does it relate to what I have already read? What is the main idea the author is trying to get across? What are two supporting details?)
D	Draw an answer	Draw a picture or diagram which answers the questions you have asked yourself.

Teaching Example

Present to students with a piece of written material, asking them to try to remember what they've read. The next day, ask them to answer comprehension questions based on this piece of written material. Keep scores of their performance. The next day, ask them to answer comprehension questions based on this piece of written material. Keep scores of their performance. After RAD has been taught, students are given another piece of written material and asked to RAD it. The comprehension questions are asked again the next day. A comparison of scores should illustrate for students the effectiveness of RAD for improving both comprehension and retention.

(Source: Kris Sanotti, St Xavier's School, Gunnedah)

13. ROSES

MATHS WORD PROBLEMS STRATEGY

Purpose of Strategy

The purpose of this strategy is to assist students systematically solve mathematical problems expressed in words. It helps students to change maths problems expressed in different words into a number sentence which they can then solve using previously mastered techniques.

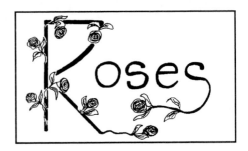

Description of Strategy

This is a • Task specific,
            • Primary strategy

R	Read	Read the problem to yourself.
O	Organise	Organise the information contained in the paragraph. What is important? What do I deal with first?
S	Select	Select the appropriate operation. Add? Subtract? Divide? Multiply?
E	Estimate	Estimate the answer you might get.
S	Solve	Solve the problem.

Teaching Example

A picture of a rose could initially be displayed in the classroom to prompt appropriate strategy use.

This could be taught after a first letter mnemonic strategy is learned so that students are familiar with the process of learning and retaining steps.

(Source: Tracey Moroney, Cathy Ogilvy, Lisa McSweeney, St Edward's School, Tamworth)

14. MFS

SELF-CORRECTION STRATEGY

Purpose of Strategy

The purpose of this strategy is to assist students to edit or correct their own writing. It can be used for proofreading their own writing after completion of a rough draft or for checking of other students' work prior to handing in. The strategy may also be used for proof reading essay exam questions.

Description of Strategy

This is a • Task specific,
         • Primary strategy

M	My	Missing words	Check for missing words.
F	Finished	Full Stops	Check that you have full stops at the end of sentences.
S	Story	Spelling	Check that words are spelled correctly

Students read through the piece of writing three times, checking each time for only one aspect as represented by the MFS mnemonic.

MFS is a modification of the COPS Self-correction strategy particularly suitable for younger students. It includes two forms of mnemonics.

Teaching Example

This strategy could be introduced to a class or individual students who do not effectively edit or conference drafts of written work. 'Before' and 'after' examples of written work corrected before introduction of MFS could be compared with examples of work corrected using the MFS strategy. The teacher should draw students' attention to the degree of improvement in written work following use of the MFS strategy.

(Source: Joel Strachan and Kris Sanotti, St Xavier's School, Gunnedah)

15.FEND

CHILD PROTECTION STRATEGY

Purpose of Strategy

The purpose of this strategy is to provide a list of techniques which can be used by children in situations where they feel uncomfortable being with an adult.

Description of Strategy

This is a • Task specific,
                  • Primary strategy

This is not a sequential strategy, each of the four elements represents an alternative course of action for the child. In situations where children feel uncomfortable in the presence of an adult, they choose an alternative from the FEND list.

F	Fight	Physically defend yourself. Yell and scream.
E	Exit	Leave the uncomfortable situation, get away.
N	Network	Create a network of five people that you can talk to. These people do not necessarily have to live in the same place as you.
D	Distract	Divert the adult's attention away from yourself.

Teaching Example

This strategy can be developed during Child Protection units. Students would use the strategy to develop four methods to be used to protect themselves and to avoid abuse and assault. Students' four methods would be listed in the FEND order to facilitate easy recall.

Note: Students must understand the 'network' concept. This could be taught using a memory strategy where nominated people are assigned to a finger. (eg; thumb—Dad, first finger—Mum, second finger—Susan, third finger—Miss Sophie etc)

(Source: Kris Sanotti, St Edward's School, Tamworth)

16. SPOT

SOCIAL PROBLEM SOLVING STRATEGY

Purpose of Strategy

The purpose of this strategy is to provide a framework for systematically analysing a social problem and identify possible solutions.

Description of Strategy

This is a • General,
      • Support strategy

Students identify aspects of a social situation which is causing them a problem using the SPOT mnemonic, possibly in conjunction with a chart listing the SPOT steps.

S	Setting	Who's involved? what are you doing? where does it take place? When does it take place?
P	Problem	What's the situation to be solved?
O	Order of action	What happened?
T	Tail end	What can be done next time? What are some possible solutions?

Teaching Example

As the day progresses, the teacher may become aware of problem involving students' social interaction (classroom or playground). Initially SPOT is presented in a general manner such as 'Suppose two students were annoying each other. I'm going to show you a way to think about and possible solve this problem'. Teacher then presents the SPOT strategy using a 'think-aloud' procedure.

When the next student interaction problem arises, either with the class or on an individual basis, have the students discuss and complete their own SPOT chart.

17.SPEW

SOCIAL PROBLEM SOLVING STRATEGY

Purpose of Strategy

The purpose of this strategy is to provide a framework for systematically analysing a social problem and identify possible solutions.

Description of Strategy

This is a • General,
          • Support strategy

Students identify aspects of a social situation which is causing them a problem using the SPEW mnemonic, possibly in conjunction with a chart listing the SPEW steps.

SPEW is a modification of the SPOT Social Problem Solving Strategy.

S	Setting	Who's involved? what are you doing? where does it take place? When does it take place?
P	Problem	What's the situation to be solved?
E	Effects of the problem	How did it make you feel?
W	What?	What would you like to have happen now or next time? What are some possible solutions?

Teaching Example

As the day progresses, the teacher may become aware of problem involving students' social interaction (classroom or playground). Initially SPEW is presented in a general manner such as 'Suppose two students were annoying each other. I'm going to show you a way to think about and possible solve this problem.' Teacher then presents the SPEW strategy using a 'think-aloud' procedure.

When the next student interaction problem arises, either with the class or on an individual basis, have the students discuss and complete their own SPEW chart.

(Source: Craig McFadden, St Carthage's School, Lismore)

PHASE TWO INSTRUCTION

In Phase Two instruction, students are taught for transfer of strategies. This Phase is one of the defining features of the SPELT approach and critical to the development of independent and interdependent learners. It builds on strategy use developed in Phase One and provides a bridge by which students can reach the third and final Phase in the SPELT instructional model. Teaching students a range of strategies and ways to use them can be actually counter-productive if students are not able to have some personal input to the structure of those strategies and the conditions under which they may be used.

Figure 5: Examples of Strategy Modification in Phase Two

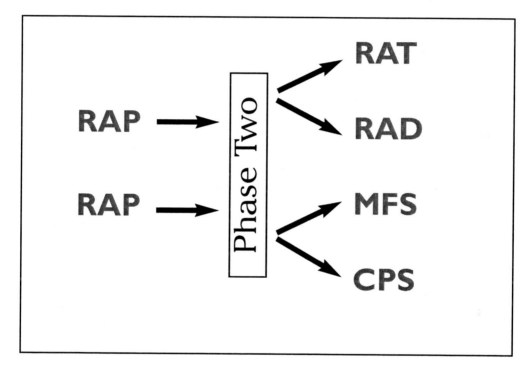

The Goals of Phase Two
Students will:

- Maintain strategy use developed in Phase One.
- Be able to evaluate their present strategy use.
- Become proficient at adapting, modifying, and/or extending strategies to different settings, situations and subject material.
- Be actively involved and interactive in the learning process

What this means for student and teacher
- Maintain strategy use developed in Phase One.

  Students need to continue using strategies explicitly taught in Phase One. The teacher may need to prompt strategy use in a range of different ways, such as by using charts, strategy 'banks', diagrams/pictures etc.

- Be able to evaluate their present strategy use.

  It is not enough for students to continue using strategies in a passive way. Teachers explicitly instruct students in ways to evaluate the strategies they are currently using. By systematically evaluating their own strategy use, students are encouraged to become more aware of their own learning and critical of the ways they perform different tasks.

- Become proficient at adapting, modifying, and/or extending strategies to different settings, situations and subject material.

  Once students have evaluated their own strategy use, they then need to act on that information. Teachers need to stress that students are increasingly responsible for their own learning; that strategies may be useful for some students but not others, and may be useful in some situations but not in others. In this Phase students change strategies learned in Phase One or already known, in order to make them more efficient or to adapt them to new situations.

- Be actively involved and interactive in the learning process

  Again, as in Phase One, students must be cognitively active participants in their own learning; comparing new and existing knowledge, practicing new strategies, constructing new understandings.

Phase Two Instructional Methods

There are several instructional methods which can be used in this Phase. They may be used separately or in conjunction with each other. Because this is a transition Phase, instructional methods require the teacher to balance explicit instruction in ways to evaluate, modify, and extend strategies with instruction which allows students to take greater control of their own learning.

1. PMI

PLUS, MINUS, INTERESTING

The PMI strategy, essentially a brainstorming activity which can be used to explore any topic in depth, is used in Phase Two as an instructional method in which students are explicitly taught how to analyse and evaluate a known strategy. It would be expected that this strategy would have been introduced and practiced as part of Phase One instruction.

Step One		Students divide a page into three columns labelled P, M, and I.
Step Two	P	Students are instructed to direct their attention to the positive (plus) aspects of the target strategy. As many positive aspects as possible are generated and listed in the P column. Points raised are to be accepted without judgement.
Step Three	M	Students are instructed to direct their attention to the negative (minus) aspects of the target strategy. As many negative aspects as possible are generated and listed in the N column. Points raised are to be accepted without judgement.
Step Four	I	Students are instructed to direct their attention to the interesting (I) aspects of the target strategy. These are aspects of the strategy which, while not necessarily being either positive or negative, the students find interesting. As many interesting aspects as possible are generated and listed in the I column. Points raised are to be accepted without judgement.
Step Five		Following generation of these three aspects, students are encouraged to discuss features of the strategy; its effectiveness, range of applications etc. Socratic Dialogue may be used to facilitate this discussion.
Step Six		Students may choose to modify the strategy; adapting or deleting aspects of the strategy identified in the M column, maximising or including aspects identified in the P and I columns.

What this Means for Student and Teacher

Students may use the PMI strategy either as individuals, part of a small group, or members of a whole class. If PMI is used individually or in small groups, points raised should be shared with the rest of the class as this allows students to see how others think. Students should be encouraged to make modifications to strategies as they apply to different situations and settings.

In this Phase of instruction, the heterogeneous nature of the class should be acknowledged. It is important to realise that while some students will wish to make changes to the target strategy to suit their own situation, other students will not wish to make any changes. Teachers must develop in students the belief that they are responsible for their own learning. Active involvement in the process of personalising strategies is one way to do this and can prove highly motivating for students.

(Source: Adapted from de Bono, 1973.)

2. PAIRED

PROBLEM SOLVING

In this method, students in pairs (problem solver, recorder) solve a problem while using a 'think-aloud' procedure. Use of this procedure enables the thinking steps used to solve the problem to be viewed, analysed and evaluated.

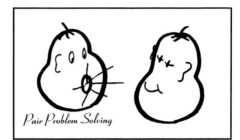

Pair Problem Solving

Step One	Problem solver applies a strategy taught in Phase One to a new or novel subject area and 'thinks aloud' while using this strategy.
Step Two	Recorder listens carefully, noting steps taken in the application of the strategy or solving of the problem. Particular attention should be paid to the recording of modifications/extensions of the target strategy generated in its new application. At the end of this 'think-aloud' procedure, the recorder may ask clarification questions of the problem solver and/or may point out errors made in the problem solving process.
Step Three	Roles are reversed, repeating Steps One and Two with the same strategy.
Step Four	Both students discuss modifications/extensions to the target strategy, seeking to document the best 'modified' strategy.

What this Means for Student and Teacher

As for the PMI method, the teacher must acknowledge that modifications made to strategies will vary according to the individual needs of students. It is not necessary that pairs of students agree on a 'best' modification. Rather, it is important to stress flexibility and encourage students to make modifications that meet their own learning needs.

(Source: Adapted from Whimbey and Lochhead, 1979.)

3. SOCRATIC

DIALOGUE

This method of instruction is a form of discussion involving an interactive relationship between teacher and student in which the teacher leads the student, through questioning, to discover for him/herself. The central concept is for the teacher to act as a catalyst forcing students to reason for themselves.

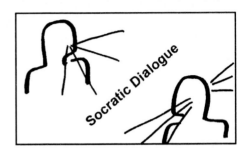

The following guidelines may be used during Socratic Dialogue:

- Start with what is known.
- Ask for multiple reasons.
- Ask for intermediate steps in the student's reasoning.
- Form general rules from specific cases.
- Pick a counter example when an insufficient reason is given.
- Pick an extreme case to illustrate a misapplication of what was stated.
- Probe for differences between two cases.
- Ask for a prediction.

This process should lead to students being able to modify, extend and apply strategies directly taught in Phase One to many and varied situations and settings. The guidelines provided above are intended to demonstrate how the process of generalisation with students can be facilitated.

There are several key teacher behaviours which are recommended to enhance the effectiveness of Socratic Dialogue. These are:

- provide silent wait-time (approx 5–10 seconds) for students' replies after questions are asked. This should allow for reflective introspection by students. Immediate responses should not be expected or promoted. Try not to provide answers to your students;
- accept and build upon students' responses;
- integrate students' responses with other information;
- extend ideas presented by the student;
- assist in clarification of students' responses, either by own questions, or by encouraging peers to ask questions such as 'what did you mean?', or by encouraging students to provide their own clarifications;
- add supplementary information either directly or by encouraging contributions from other students.

What this Means for Student and Teacher

In Phase Two instruction, Socratic Dialogue should lead students to derive general principles from the specific strategy taught and to apply the general principles learned to new settings and materials. An important caution regarding use of this method must be observed; Socratic Dialogue should not be used when introducing new concepts as its central assumption is that the required knowledge is already possessed by the learner. It is, however, a very powerful method for helping students develop links and examine interrelationships between concepts and develop conclusions and general principles.

Thinking Aloud

Described by Meichenbaum and Goodman (1971), 'thinking aloud' means precisely what it says. When using this technique, the student or teacher attempts to put into words all the things going on in their head. This might involve the procedures being used to complete a task, the 'incidental' thoughts going on, reminders of strategies to be used, thoughts about feeling or affect. This is an extremely useful technique for both learner and teacher.

An example presented by these authors refers to a learner copying a picture from a model:

> Okay, what is it I have to do? You want me to copy the picture with different lines, I have to go slowly and carefully. Okay, draw the line down, down, good: then to the right, that's it; now down some more and to the left. Good, I'm doing fine so far. remember to go slowly.
> Now back up again. No! I was supposed to go down. That's okay. Just erase the line carefully... good. Even if I make an error I can go on slowly and carefully. I have to go down now. Finished. I did it!

The thinking in this example can be categorised in the following way and serves several functions:

Problem definition 'What is it I have to do? You want me to copy the picture with different lines.'

Focusing attention and response guidance 'I have to go slowly and carefully. Okay, draw the line down'

Self-reinforcement 'Good, I'm doing fine so far.'

Self-evaluative coping skills and error-correcting options 'That's okay. Just erase the line carefully... good. Even if I make an error I can go on slowly and carefully.'

PHASE THREE INSTRUCTION

The Goals of Phase Three

Students will:

- Monitor, evaluate and generate effective and efficient strategies to aid their own acquisition, thinking about, retention, and retrieval of the material to be learned.
- Be actively involved and interactive in the learning process

What this Means for Student and Teacher

Students will:

- Monitor, evaluate and generate effective and efficient strategies to aid their own acquisition, thinking about, retention, and retrieval of the material to be learned.

  Students continue to monitor and evaluate current strategy use in the same way as they did in Phase Two. The distinguishing feature of this Phase is that students are now able to generate new strategies to aid learning.

- Be actively involved and interactive in the learning process

  As they have throughout the instructional model, students must continue to be cognitively active participants in their own learning; comparing new and existing knowledge, practicing new strategies, constructing new understandings.

Phase Three Instructional Methods

In this Phase of the SPELT instructional sequence, students are taking greater control for their own learning. This Phase is, therefore, meant to be much more flexible than either Phases One or Two. A problem solving approach is taken in which the teacher creatively interacts with students, constantly emphasising and helping them to see the process they are using while learning.

Teachers in this Phase should not only use good teaching techniques but should explicitly describe to students what they are doing and why. This information can then be used by students as a framework for generation of their own learning strategies.

General Problem Solving Lesson Format

Step One	Presentation of a task with minimal teacher guidance
Step Two	Analysis of how the task was completed
Step Three	Generation of a strategy or strategies used
Step Four	Evaluation of the effectiveness of the generated strategies leading to further refinement.
Step Five	Practice using generated strategies encouraging personal modification.

Paired Problem Solving (Phase III)

This method, a version of which may be also used in Phase Two, involves students in pairs (problem solver, recorder) solving a problem while using a 'think-aloud' procedure. Use of this procedure enables the thinking steps used to solve the problem to be viewed, analysed and evaluated.

Step One	Problem solver solves a new problem presented by the teacher without a given strategy and 'thinks aloud' while solving the problem. Problem solver will either choose a known strategy from their repertoire, modify a known strategy, or generate a new one.
Step Two	Recorder listens carefully, noting strategy used and steps taken in the solving of the problem. At the end of this 'think-aloud' procedure, the recorder may ask clarification questions of the problem solver and/or may point out errors made in the problem solving process.
Step Three	Roles are reversed, repeating Steps One and Two with the same strategy.
Step Four	Both students discuss strategy used or developed, possibly seeking to document and present a 'new' strategy.

Socratic Dialogue (Phase III)

This method of instruction can be used in the same manner in Phases Two and Three. It is a form of discussion involving an interactive relationship between teacher and student in which the teacher leads the student, through questioning, to discover for him/herself. The central concept is for the teacher to act as a catalyst forcing students to reason for themselves.

The following guidelines may be used during Socratic Dialogue;

- Start with what is known.
- Ask for multiple reasons.
- Ask for intermediate steps in the student's reasoning.
- Form general rules from specific cases.
- Pick a counter example when an insufficient reason is given.
- Pick an extreme case to illustrate a misapplication of what was stated.
- Probe for differences between two cases.
- Ask for a prediction.

This process should lead to students being able to identify general learning principles and generate effective and efficient learning strategies.

There are several key teacher behaviours which are recommended to enhance the effectiveness of Socratic Dialogue.

- provide silent wait-time (approx 5–10 seconds) for students' replies after questions are asked. This should allow for reflective introspection by students. Immediate responses should not be expected or promoted. Try not to provide answers to your students.

- accept and build upon students' responses
- integrate students' responses with other information
- extend ideas presented by the student
- assist in clarification of students' responses, either by own questions, or by encouraging peers to ask questions such as 'what did you mean?', or by encouraging students to provide their own clarifications
- add supplementary information either directly or by encouraging contributions from other students.

What this Means for Student and Teacher

In Phase Three instruction, Socratic Dialogue should lead students to derive general principles from the specific strategy taught and to apply the general principles to the generation of new strategies.

Thinking Aloud

Described by Meichenbaum and Goodman (1971), 'thinking aloud' means precisely what it says. When using this technique, the student or teacher attempts to put into words all the things going on in their head. This might involve the procedures being used to complete a task, the 'incidental' thoughts going on, reminders of strategies to be used, thoughts about feeling or affect. This is an extremely useful technique for both learner and teacher.

An example presented by these authors refers to a learner copying a picture from a model:

> Okay, what is it I have to do? You want me to copy the picture with different lines, I have to go slowly and carefully. Okay, draw the line down, down, good: then to the right, that's it; now down some more and to the left. Good, I'm doing fine so far. remember to go slowly.
>
> Now back up again. No! I was supposed to go down. That's okay. Just erase the line carefully… good. Even if I make an error I can go on slowly and carefully. I have to go down now. Finished. I did it!

A GUIDED INTERNALITY TEACHING PERSPECTIVE

As an internal locus of control orientation promotes students' active involvement and independence in learning, a teaching perspective of guided internality (using the concept of dual control for students to move them by providing positive external assistance toward internality, especially those displaying learned helplessness) was generated to assist teachers in empowering learners (Knight, 1991; 1994). Such empowerment promotes students' self-management and independence, thereby encouraging their active participation in the learning process

Guided internality is a teaching perspective which can be applied to all instructional areas encouraging students to become active learners and thereby reinforce their beliefs in realistic personal control. This perspective provides direction for teaching-learning situations with the teacher's role being to guide students and emphasise to them the management of their own learning. As students take more responsibility for their learning the teacher is to phase out the guiding cues, with the degree of intervention depending upon students' abilities, characteristics and situational contexts.

In other words, internal locus of control and positive external support from the teacher acting as a facilitator encourages students to take responsibility for their behaviour with regard to the development of learning skills. For example, a student reading a passage may require positive external support from the teacher in the form exposure to a list of sight vocabulary and modelling of the 'read-on' strategy to successfully read the passage. As the student gains confidence with his/her reading, direct positive external support can be phased out and indirect support provided by choosing texts at an appropriate level for the student.

The outline that follows addresses aspects of the environment and a teacher's role as they relate to effective implementation of guided internality.

Classroom Environment

The classroom environment should be structured to help students acquire skills to become increasingly self-responsible for their learning. It is important that the environment offer an atmosphere where the teacher encourages internal discipline while maintaining an amount of external discipline conducive to an effective learning situation. A non-threatening climate of trust, where students have the freedom to move about, interact with others and explore the environment, should be established. The rules and guidelines for operating in the classroom should be jointly discussed by teachers and students so that students have an active role in negotiating classroom expectations. Such a shared role then encourages students to accept responsibility for their actions in the environment. The environment is now structured in such a way that allows the SPELT instructional model to be effectively implemented.

Teacher's Role

The guided internality teaching perspective provides direction for teaching-learning situations with the teacher's role being to guide students and emphasise to them the management of their own learning. Specifically, it is important when using guided internality that teachers:

- Teach the 'What', 'When', 'Why' and 'How' of the strategy.
- Model strategy training and make their thought processes overt.
- Give students sufficient practice in using strategies to ensure mastery of the strategies.
- Reinforce the need for effort in the form of attentiveness to the strategy. It is of no value to tell students to go away and try harder or study more. Effort alone is useless without strategic knowledge.
- Encourage students to accept responsibility for their own learning with failure attributed to the lack of effort or the use of an inefficient strategy.
- Promote students' active role in the learning process by encouraging them to make decisions, set realistic goals and take risks.
- Remember that competitive tasks are more likely to produce maladaptive

attributions then cooperative tasks.

- Role-play different scenarios that manipulate the degree of causation for events, thus reinforcing the development of an internal LOC through dual control and teaching that behaviour is controllable. Teachers need to be aware that they cannot change students attributions overnight and that attribution retraining needs to be intensive, prolonged and consistent.
- Initially, teachers need to focus on task specific beliefs to move away from global feelings of learned helplessness.
- Focus on informational feedback that examines the effectiveness of strategies.
- Match strategies to students' cognitive abilities.
- Acknowledge the bidirectional relationship between metacognitive knowledge and motivational factors.

Section Three

In this section we shall examine some aspects of the implementation of SPELT in schools and school systems.

EFFECTIVENESS OF *SPELT*

A three year longitudinal study in Canada (Mulcahy, 1991; Mulcahy *et al.*, 1989) was conducted to evaluate the effectiveness of SPELT by comparing it to another learning and thinking program known as Instrumental Enrichment (IE) (Feurerstein, Rand, Hoffman and Miller, 1980) and a control group receiving normal instruction. The goal of both programs is to enhance students' thinking so that they become more active, independent thinkers and problem solvers. However, while SPELT is embedded directly in curriculum content, IE is considered as a detached program because it is firstly taught separate from classroom content before being integrated into the curriculum at a later stage.

The effectiveness of SPELT and IE programs were compared to a control group for three groups of 300 students (gifted, average and learning disabled). Initially, the students were in grade 4 (progressing to grade 6) and grade 7 (progressing to grade 9) over the course of the study. After inservicing, teachers taught the programs for two years followed by a maintenance year where no strategy based instruction occurred.

The objectives of the research were:

- To assess the effectiveness of the programs in relation to their impact upon students' achievement (reading, mathematics), motivation and cognitive ability. Teachers, administrators, parents and students' perceptions of the programs were also collected;
- To examine the effects on the different learning groups of gifted, average and learning disabled students;
- To assess the feasibility of implementing strategies on a larger scale and as part of schools' curricula;
- To identify methods of inservicing teachers to ensure effective implementation in schools.

The results of the research were very promising, especially for gifted (enjoying the challenge of extending and generating their own strategies) and learning disabled students (having strategies for the first time). It is believed that relatively little change initially for the average group was due to the fact that these students were already using strategies, albeit not in the most effective ways. Generally, application of the SPELT program produced more positive and longer lasting changes than the other groups (Mulcahy, 1991).

Perceptions of SPELT teachers, administrators and parents were also positive. Teachers reported that students were more willing to tackle tasks, were more involved by asking more questions and were encouraged to persevere at tasks. Of these teachers, 85% were still using aspects of the SPELT program two years after the study had been completed. Parents also noted that their children were more confident and had more self-esteem.

Overall, it can be claimed that SPELT has the potential to make enduring positive changes for students' learning and problem solving skills.

INCORPORATING SPELT INTO SCHOOLS

So now we've reached the situation where you are interested in adopting SPELT for your classroom or school. It has been well established, however, that 'one shot' professional development rarely brings about fundamental change in a person's teaching methods. Usually a new approach involves teachers in substituting new strategies and methods into pre-existing theoretical frameworks. It is relatively easy to convince schools and educational systems of the benefits of such a program as SPELT. However, to see real change evidenced by changes in classroom practice embedded in a school culture is much more of a challenge. How can an educational initiative such as the SPELT professional development program for class teachers be further shaped and refined to ensure that real (not superficial) change is visible in classroom practice and therefore student outcomes. Structures need to be set up that support teachers and students as they attempt to bring about changes in their thinking and practice.

Whether teachers will accept and implement SPELT very much depends on their individual starting points and their commitment to it (Do they feel comfortable with the type of teaching style being advocated? Are they already experienced with this style? What skills do they already have? What stage are they at in their career? What is their sense of efficacy regarding change-Can they do it? Are concrete examples of how to do it provided for teachers? Does the principal and school executive understand what is trying to be achieved?

Critical factors involved in sustained change include: major stakeholders owning the implementation, including such aspects as developing policy on implementation; staff identifying their needs (both personal and student needs); and the identification of problems (and solutions).

More specifically:

- at what level will SPELT be adopted- system/school/area/classroom level?

- is participation by teachers voluntary?

- begin with a contained and consistent focus for implementation of strategies by all participants (eg CARING as a listening strategy for the whole school, if this is the level of involvement);

- encouragement of continued use and open communication by, for example, establishing a SPELT spot at every staff meeting which encourages open communication and problem-solving. Gathering information and being able to problem solve with others during implementation is critical to effective implementation.

- using a common structure across the school for indicating strategies taught to the whole class, what was effective with at risk, gifted and talented students etc;

- descriptions of tasks that indicate use of strategies and development;

- extra support needed (eg resources, professional development etc);

- monitoring progress as part of the school plan-what performance indicators will indicate school implementation of strategies?

Actions to Assist Real Change

- Whole school commitment is best. Implementation at a whole school level will more than likely fail if it is too dependent upon an individual not receiving support and encouragement at the whole school level.

- Involve parents by informing them of the SPELT approach and its usefulness to parents in dealing with practical home-based situations such as coping with issues like homework and the completion of projects.

- Establishing teacher commitment to the package and importantly its philosophy as a critical element in change

- As teachers gain more experience with SPELT the more it is subsumed into their practice, and therefore the more it will be effectively used.

Remember that effective implementation of SPELT takes time. Do you have a timeline drawn up? We can't really predict what the changes will be and no specific time frame can be stated. Remember to start small and experiment gradually and don't give in to early failures. You will find that some things work with some students and not with others. You should aim to build up a repertoire of successful strategies and practices.

Some Teaching Tips

- Don't ignore the motivational components of strategy instruction.

- Have students practice the use of the strategies and embed this practice in easy content (PHASE I).

- Integrate strategies with what students already know (PHASE I).

- Encourage students to evaluate the effectiveness of the strategies they use (PHASE II).

- Don't teach too many strategies at one time as this may lead to student overload.

Personal Questions for You to Consider About SPELT

- Will it address my needs? Will it be of use to me as a classroom teacher? school counsellor? school principal?

- How do I have to change?

  - Teaching style?
  - Time? How achievable is implementation? Do I have to neglect anything that I currently teach?
  - Are new skills needed? Is all my previous teaching experience wasted?
  - Priority? Is it high on my list of needs? What's in it for me?
  - Am I motivated and committed to do this?

- What will it do for my students?

  - Skills?
  - Motivation?
  - Self-Esteem?
  - Independence?

- What support will I get in the form of time to implement, special conditions and resources?

- What resources will I need?

Personal Action Program for the Introduction of Spelt

What actions do you propose to take following this presentation?

_____

_____

_____

_____

What problems do you foresee?

_____

_____

_____

_____

How will you overcome these problems?

_____

_____

_____

_____

How will you judge the success of these actions and this presentation?

_____

_____

_____

_____

Construct a time-line indicating the implementation of SPELT.

_____

_____

_____

_____

THE SPELT PROGRAM WORKSHOPS

A two day workshop provides training for implementing a metacognitive and cognitive strategies instruction approach entitled S.P.E.L.T. (Strategies Program for Effective Learning/Thinking) developed by Professor Mulcahy and colleagues in Canada. This approach has been extensively evaluated in Canada with very impressive results and is currently being developed in other parts of the world including Australia, New Zealand, U.S.A., India and South Korea.

The major goal of the approach is to develop students (K-12) who are more: active learners, thinkers and problem solvers; independent, planful and strategically efficient in their approach to learning; aware of, and better able to control their own thinking. It is therefore relevant to all classrooms which attempt to cater for the range of children's abilities from those with learning difficulties through to the gifted and talented.

The approach is designed to teach cognitive and metacognitive strategies utilising the content of the regular curriculum and it is applicable to infants, primary and high school classrooms.

A variety of cognitive and metacognitive strategies are integrated into the approach, including strategies that are effective for remembering information, comprehending information, communicating information, controlling emotion and motivation as well as general and specific problem solving. A 250–page teachers inservice manual has been developed which provides the theoretical background as well as explicit information on the different strategies along with ideas on how to teach them.

The workshop involves an introduction to the program's theoretical framework in cognitive psychology, to its three phase instructional approach and the systematic transfer of students' strategic repertoire established to other situations, settings and applications. The workshop is designed to allow teachers to experience first hand the process that parallels what their students will undergo as the approach is implemented in their classrooms.

References

Alley, G. and D. Deshler 1979, *Teaching the Learning Disabled Adolescent: Strategies and Methods*, Love Publishing, Denver.

Ashman, A. and R. Conway 1989, *Cognitive Strategies for Special Education*, Routledge, London.

Biggs, J. and R. Telfer, 1987, *The Process of Learning* (3rd ed.), Prentice Hall, Sydney.

Borkowski, J., M. Carr, E. Rellinger and M. Pressley, 1991, 'Self-regulated Cognition: Interdependence of Metacognition, Attributions and Self-esteem', in B.F. Jones and L. Idol (eds.), *Dimensions of Thinking and Cognitive Instruction*, North Central Regional Educational Laboratory, NJ.

Dansereau, D. 1985, 'Learning Strategy Research', in J. Segal, S. Chipman and R. Glaser (eds). *Thinking and Learning Skills, Volume 1: Relating Instruction to Research*, Erlbaum, Hillsdale.

de Bono, E. 1973, *CoRT Thinking Materials*, Direct Education Services, London.

Feurerstein, R., Y. Rand, M. Hoffman and R. Miller 1980, *Instrumental Enrichment: An Intervention Program for Cognitive Modifiability*, University Park Press, Baltimore.

Fullan, M. 1991, *The New Meaning of Educational Change* (2nd ed), Teachers College Press, New York.

Halmhuber, N and S. Paris, 1993, 'Perceptions of Competence and Control and the Use of Coping Strategies by Children with Disabilities', *Learning Disabilities Quarterly*, 16, pp.93–111.

Harris, K.R. and M. Pressley, 1991, 'The Nature of Cognitive Strategy Instruction: Interactive Strategy Construction', *Exceptional Children*, 58, pp.393–403.

Knight B.A. 1991, 'A Teaching Perspective of Guided Internality Relevant to Teachers of Intellectually Disabled Students', Proceedings of the 15th National Special Education Conference, September, pp.241–245.

—— 1993, 'Using a Guided Internality Teaching Perspective to Promote Learning Disabled Students' Active Involvement in Learning', *Australian Journal of Remedial Education*, 25, pp.22–23.

—— 1994, 'Literacy: Active learning for Teachers and Students', *Reading*, 28(3), pp.30–33.

—— 1995, 'The Influence of Locus of Control on Gifted and Talented Students', *Gifted Education International*, 11(1), pp.31–33.

—— 1997, 'Supporting Students' Literacy Development in the Secondary School', *Australian Journal of Learning Disabilities*, 2(3), pp.21–24

Knight, B.A. and D. Paterson 1994, 'Developing Autonomous Learners : Implications for Schools', *Independent Education*, 24(2), pp.27–31.

——1996, 'A Longitudinal study of Cognitive and Metacognitive Instruction in Elementary Classrooms', paper presented at the 54th Annual Convention of the International Council of Psychologists, Banff, Canada.

Meichenbaum, D. H. and J. Goodman, 1971, 'Training Impulsive Children to Talk to Themselves: A Means of Developing Self-control', *Journal of Abnormal Psychology*, 77(2), pp.115–26.

Mulcahy, R. 1991, 'Developing Autonomous Learners', *Alberta Journal of Educational Research*, 38(4), pp.385–397.

Mulcahy, R., D. Peat, I. Andrews, L. Clifford, K. Marfo and S. Cho 1989, *Cognitive Education Project: Final Report*, Alberta Education, Government of Alberta, Canada.

Mulcahy, R., K. Marfo, D. Peat and J. Andrews 1984, *A Strategies Program for Effective/Learning Thinking: A Teachers' Manual*, University of Alberta, Edmonton.

Mulcahy, R. and W. Wiles 1996. 'A Metacognitive Instructional Approach for Developing Self-directed Learners', *The Journal of the Research Institute of Korean Education*, 11.

Rigney, J. W. 1978, 'Learning Strategies: A Theoretical Perspective', in H. O'Neil (ed.), *Learning Strategies*, Academic Press, New York.

Rotheram, M. J. 1978, 'Social Skills Training Program Elementary and High School Classrooms', paper presented at 7th Annual Behaviour Therapy Association Conference, Houston, Texas.

Rotter, J.B. 1990, 'Internal Versus External Control of Reinforcement: A Case History of a Variable', *American Psychologist*, 45, pp.489–493.

Sternberg, R.J. 1986, *Intelligence Applied: Understanding and Increasing Your Intellectual Skills*, Harcourt Brace Javanovich, Toronto.

Vygotsky, L. 1978, *Mind in Society*, Cambridge University Press, Cambridge.

Whimbey, A. and J. Lochhead 1979, *Problem Solving and Comprehension*, Franklin Institute Press, Philadelphia.

Wong, P.T.P., and C.F. Sproule, 1984, 'An Attributional Analysis of the Locus of Control Construct', in H.M. Lefcourt (ed.), *Research with the Locus of Control Construct: Volume 3. Extensions and Limitations*, Academic Press, New York, pp.309–360.